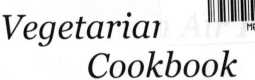

Vegetarian Air Fryer Cookbook

The Ultimate High-Tech Yet Simple Way to Enjoy Healthy Food While Staying on a Budget with VEGETARIAN Recipes that Even Beginners Can Prepare

Chef Max Wilbur

Table of Contents

INTRODUCTION

The Air Fryer Oven Grill is the perfect addition to any kitchen. It's a modern and stylish countertop cooking appliance that cooks faster and more efficiently than your standard electric or gas grill. It can be used on its own as a small griller or in conjunction with your larger countertop oven as an air fryer.

The Air Fryer Grill has a unique design that allows you to cook a wide range of foods that your traditional stovetop or electric grills cannot handle. The large handle and spacious cooking area make it an attractive choice for anyone who wants to save time and space in your kitchen.

Step By Step Directions to Use the Air Fryer Grill

Step one:

Preheat the air fryer, add desired foods to the basket and close the lid. Turn the vent control knob to the "AIR DRY" position. Set the timer to cook for 20 minutes at 400°F (200°C). To use as a crockpot, set on low heat and cook for 8 hours or overnight.

Step two:

Remove food from the basket, drain excess oil, and serve. You may also season or marinate for further flavor enhancement before cooking (optional).

After cooking, keep calm in a covered container until ready to eat.

For best results, does not freeze or store in the refrigerator for longer than three days (if possible), as this will remove some of the oils from foods.

If you must store longer, at a low temperature (50 – 60 and use within 2-4 days. You may also season or marinate for further flavor enhancement before cooking (optional).

Tips and Tricks for Using the Air Fryer Grill

Use fresh ingredients that produce less moisture - consider no-oil salads or sautéed vegetables instead of fried.

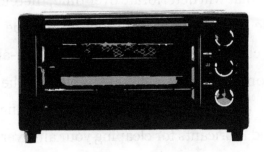

Care and maintenance

For best results, never immerse or submerge air fryer in water or any other liquid during use. Avoid letting water get on the heating element or fan, as this can cause damage to these parts and may affect their performance over time. There are no moving parts that will deteriorate over time; therefore, cleaning all removable parts will only require that they be wiped clean with a damp cloth. Use the only high-quality non-abrasive mild cleaner on non-removable components such as the door gasket or drip tray, as this can affect their performance. Use only silicone-based lubricants for cleaning your air fryer grill; do not use aerosol sprays in this area as these can damage delicate internal components. Avoid touching metal surfaces inside the appliance with your hands, as this can result in skin rashes or other issues

Use only mild dish detergent and hot water on a soft sponge to improve the longevity of the machine's finish.

It can cook up to 10 pounds of food in just 8 minutes!

The device cooks food by circulating air around the food. In just 30 minutes, you can have a delicious meal like never before. There are no dirty pans to clean and no wasted oil, making this device a win-win for both your health and your budget.

It is a tool that will revolutionize the way you cook. Unbox, prepare and start cooking.

The air fryer grill is easy to use, with the LCD panel on its side shows you the time and temperature settings. You can set up 8 different modes to cook your favorite foods. If you only want 2 minutes per side, use that mode; if you prefer 4 minutes per side, use that mode; if you wish to 6 minutes cooking time per side, then use the extended cooking mode.

Its 4 heat settings make sure your food doesn't burn before cooking is completed. It also has a power outlet to plug in your device and keep it safe from electricity spikes or power surges during those hot summer days. The food inside the air fryer cannot burn because of the non-stick pan plates used to make sure no oil gets on the food as you are cooking.

It also has a cool-touch exterior so that kids can use this without worry about burning their hands on the hot pan surface. The glass lid can be opened after it has been cooked so you can serve it in a bowl or plate without having to wait for the cool-down of the unit before serving.

This device is similar to other air fryers, except for how much air it can maintain at a time. This allows for more consistent cooking and better results every time.

With your Air Fryer Grill, you can prepare meals faster than ever before. You can use almost any cooking utensil to fry, bake, roast, broil, and much more. You can create gourmet meals in a fraction of the time it takes with traditional grill cookbooks or no cookers'

This product can be used for just about any type of food you can think of, so long as you are willing to try something new. It is easy to use and easy to clean, and uniquely can be used in the oven or on your grill or stovetop. The versatility will make you think about this tool more often than it took you to learn how great it is!!

Air Fryer Cooking Times

	Temp (°F)	Time (min)		Temp (°F)	Time (min)
Vegetables					
Asparagus (sliced 1-inch)	400°F	5	**Onions** (peart)	400°F	10
Beets (whole)	400°F	40	**Parsnips**	380°F	15
Broccoli (florets)	400°F	6	**Peppers** (1-inch chunks)	400°F	15
Brussels Sprouts (halved)	380°F	15	**Potatoes** (small baby, 1.5 lbs)	400°F	15
Carrots (sliced 1/2-inch)	380°F	15	**Potatoes** (1-inch chunks)	400°F	12
Cauliflower (florets)	400°F	12	**Potatoes** (baked whole)	400°F	40
Com on the cob	390°F	6	**Squash** (1/2-inch chunks)	400°F	12
Eggplant (11/2-inch cubes)	400°F	15	**Sweet Potato**	380°F	30 to 35
Fennel (quartered)	370°F	15	**Tomatoes** (cherry)	400°F	4
Green Beans	400°F	5	**Tomatoes** (halves)	350°F	10
Kale leaves	250°F	12	**Zucchini** (1/2-inch sticks)	400°F	12
Mushrooms (sliced 1/4-inch)	400°F	5			

Chicken

Breasts, bone in (1.25 lbs.)	370°F	25	**Legs, bone in** (1.75 lbs.)	380°F	30
Breasts, boneless (4 oz.)	380°F	12	**Wings** (2 lbs.)	400°F	12
Drumsticks (2.5 lbs.)	370°F	20	**Game Hen** (halved - 2 lbs.)	390°F	20
Thighs, bone In (2 lbs.)	380°F	22	**Whole Chicken** (6.5 lbs.)	360°F	75
Thighs, boneless (1.5 lbs.)	380°F	18 to 20	**Tenders**	360°F	8 to 10

Beef

Burger (4 oz.)	370°F	16 to 20	**Meatballs** (3-inch)	380°F	10
Filet Mignon (8 oz.)	400°F	18	**Ribeye, bone In** (1-inch, 8 oz.)	400°F	10 to 15
Flank Steak (1.5 lbs.)	400°F	12	**Sirloin steaks** (1-inch, 12 oz.)	400°F	9 to 14
London Broil (2 lbs.)	400°F	20 to 28	**Beef Eye Round Roast** (4 lbs.)	390°F	45 to 55
Meatballs (1-inch)	380°F	7			

Pork and Lamb

Loin (2 lbs.)	360°F	55	**Bacon** (thick cut)	400°F	6 to 10

Pork Chops, bone in (1-inch, 6.5 oz.)	400°F	12	**Sausages**	380°F	15
Tenderloin (1 lb.)	370°F	15	**Lamb Loin Chops** (1-	400°F	8 to 12
Bacon (regular)	400°F	5 to 7	**Rack of lamb** (1.5 - 2 lbs.)	380°F	22
Fish and Seafood					
Calamari (8 oz.)	400°F	4	**Tuna steak**	400°F	7 to 10
Fish Fillet (1-inch, 8oz.)	400°F	10	**Scallops**	400°F	5 to 7
Salmon, fillet (6oz.)	380°F	12	**Shrimp**	400°F	5
Swordfish steak	400°F	10			
Frozen Foods					
Onion Rings (12 oz.)	400°F	8	**Fish Sticks** (10 oz.)	400°F	10
Thin French Fries (20 oz.)	400°F	14	**Fish Fillets** (1/2-inch, 10	400°F	14
Thick French Fries (17 oz.)	400°F	18	**Chicken Nuggets** (12	400°F	10
Mozzarella Sticks (11 oz.)	400°F	8	**Breaded Shrimp**	400°F	9
Pot Stickers (10 oz.)	400°F	8			

Vegetarian Recipes

Vegetarian Recipes

Smoked Paprika Cauliflower Florets

Preparation time: 10 minutes

Cooking time: 20 minutes

Servings 4

Ingredients:

- 1 large head cauliflower,
- 2 teaspoons smoked paprika
- 1 teaspoon garlic powder
- Salt and freshly black pepper, to taste
- Cooking spray

Directions:

1. Spray the air fry basket with cooking spray.
2. In a medium bowl, merge the cauliflower florets with the smoked paprika and garlic powder until evenly coated. Sprinkle with salt and pepper.
3. Place the cauliflower florets in the air fry basket and lightly mist with cooking spray.
4. Place the air fry basket on the air fry position.
5. Select Air Fry, set temperature to 400F (205C), and set time to 20 minutes. Stir the cauliflower four times during cooking.
6. Remove the cauliflower from the air fryer grill and serve hot.

Nutrition: Calories 256 Fat 13.3 g Carbohydrates 0 g Sugar 0 g Protein 34.5 g Cholesterol 78 mg

Crispy Cheesy Broccoli Tots

Preparation time: 20 minutes

Cooking time: 15 minutes

Servings 4

Ingredients:

- 12 ounces (340 g) frozen broccoli, thawed, drained, and patted dry
- 1 large egg, lightly beaten
- 1/2 cup seasoned whole-wheat bread crumbs
- 1/4 cup shredded cheese
- 1/4 cup grated Parmesan cheese
- 11/2 teaspoons minced garlic
- Salt and freshly ground black pepper,
- Cooking spray

Directions:

1. Spritz the air fry basket lightly with cooking spray.
2. Bring the remaining ingredients into a food processor and process until the mixture resembles a coarse meal. Transfer the mixture to a bowl.
3. Using a tablespoon, scoop out the broccoli mixture and form into 24 oval "tater tot" shapes with your hands.
4. Put the tots in the prepared basket in a single layer, spacing them 1 inch apart. Mist the tots lightly with cooking spray.
5. Place the air fry basket on the air fry position.

6. Select Air Fry, set temperature to 375F (190C), and set time to 15 minutes. Flip the tots halfway through the cooking time.

7. When done, the tots will be lightly browned and crispy. Remove from the air fryer grill and serve on a plate.

Nutrition: Calories 304 Fat 6 g Carbohydrates 1 g Sugar 0.5 g Protein 54 g Cholesterol 152 mg

Easy Toasted Asparagus

Preparation time: 10 minutes

Cooking time: 12 minutes

Servings 4

Ingredients

- 2 pounds (907 g) asparagus, trimmed
- 3 tablespoons extra-virgin olive oil, divided
- 1 teaspoon kosher salt, divided
- 1 pint cherry tomatoes
- 4 large eggs
- 1/4 teaspoon freshly ground black pepper

Directions:

1. Put the asparagus on the sheet pan and drizzle with 2 tablespoons of olive oil, tossing to coat. Season with 1/2 teaspoon of kosher salt.

2. Place the pan on the toast position.

3. Select Toast, set temperature to 375F (190C), and set time to 12 minutes.

4. Meanwhile, set the cherry tomatoes with the remaining 1 tablespoon of olive oil in a medium bowl until well coated.

5. After 6 minutes, detach the pan and toss the asparagus. Evenly scatter the asparagus in the middle of the sheet pan. Attach the tomatoes around the perimeter of the pan. Return the pan to the air fryer grill and continue cooking.

6. After 2 minutes, remove the pan from the air fryer grill.

7. Gently crack the eggs, one at a time, over the asparagus, spacing them out. Flavor with the remaining 1/2 teaspoon of kosher salt and the pepper. Return the pan to the air fryer grill and continue cooking. Cook until the eggs are cooked to your desired doneness.

8. When done, set the asparagus and eggs among four plates. Set each plate evenly with the tomatoes and serve.

Nutrition: Calories 428 Carbohydrates 2.2 g Sugar 1.1 g Protein 27.5 g Cholesterol 113 mg

Fast Spicy Kung Pao Tofu

Preparation time: 10 minutes

Cooking time: 10 minutes

Servings 4

Ingredients:

- 1/3 cup Asian-Style sauce
- 1 teaspoon cornstarch
- 1/2 teaspoon red pepper flakes,
- 1 pound extra-firm tofu, cut into 1-inch cubes
- 1 small carrot, peeled and divide into 1/4-inch-thick coins
- 1 small green bell pepper,
- 3 scallions,
- 3 tablespoons Toasted unsalted peanuts

Directions:

1. In a large bowl, merge together the sauce, red pepper flakes, and cornstarch. Fold in the tofu, pepper, carrot, and the white parts of the scallions and toss to coat. Spread the mixture evenly on the sheet pan.

2. Place the pan on the toast position.

3. Select Toast, set temperature to 375F (190C), and set time to 10 minutes. Merge the ingredients once halfway through the cooking time.

4. When done, remove the pan from the air fryer grill. Serve.

Nutrition: Calories 356 Fat 8.7 g Carbohydrates 1.4 g Sugar 0.2 g Protein 62.2 g Cholesterol 153 mg

Easy Maple and Pecan Granola

Preparation time: 5 minutes

Cooking time: 20 minutes

Servings 4

Ingredients:

- 11/2 cups rolled oats
- 1/4 cup maple syrup
- 1/4 cup pecan pieces
- 1 teaspoon vanilla extract
- 1/2 teaspoon ground cinnamon

Directions:

1. Line a baking sheet with parchment paper.
2. Mix together the oats, pecan pieces, maple syrup, cinnamon, and vanilla in a large bowl and stir until the oats and pecan pieces are completely coated. Set the mixture evenly on the baking sheet.
3. Place the baking sheet on the bake position.
4. Select Bake, set temperature to 300F (150C), and set time to 20 minutes. Stir once halfway through the cooking time.
5. When done, remove from the air fryer grill and cool before serving.

Nutrition: Calories 290 Fat 10 g Carbohydrates 3 g Sugar 0.3 g Protein 40 g Cholesterol 0 mg

Cheesy Bean and Salsa Tacos

Preparation time: 12 minutes

Cooking time: 7 minutes

Servings 4

Ingredients:

- 1 can black beans, drained and rinsed
- 1/2 cup prepared salsa
- 11/2 teaspoons chili powder
- 4 ounces grated cheese
- 2 tablespoons minced onion
- 8 flour tortillas
- 2 tablespoons vegetable or extra-virgin olive oil
- Shredded lettuce, for serving

Directions:

1. In a medium bowl, add the beans, chili powder and salsa. Coarsely mash them with a potato masher. Fold in the onion and cheese and stir until combined.

2. Set the flour tortillas on a cutting board and spoon 2 to 3 tablespoons of the filling into each tortilla. Set the tortillas over, pressing lightly to even out the filling. Garnish the tacos on one side with half the olive oil and put them, oiled side down, on the sheet pan. Garnish the top side with the remaining olive oil.

3. Place the pan into the air fryer grill.

4. Select Air Fry, set temperature to 400F (205C), and set time to 7 minutes. Set the tacos halfway through the cooking time.

5. Remove the pan from the air fryer grill and allow to cool. Serve

Nutrition: Calories: 373 Total Fat: 21 Saturated Fat: 3g Cholesterol: 75mg Sodium: 218mg Carbohydrates: 13g Fiber: 1g Protein: 34g

Butter Toasted Cremini Mushrooms

Preparation time: 8 minutes

Cooking time: 30 minutes

Servings: 11/2 cups

Ingredients:

- 1 pound button or cremini mushrooms, washed, stems trimmed, and cut into quarters or thick slices
- 1/4 cup water
- 1 teaspoon kosher salt
- 3 tablespoons unsalted butter,

Directions:

1. Bring a large piece of aluminum foil on the sheet pan. Bring the mushroom pieces in the middle of the foil. Scatter them out into an even layer. Set the water over them, season with the salt, and add the butter. Wrap the mushrooms in the foil.

2. Place the pan on the toast position.

3. Select Toast, set the temperature to 325F (163C)

4. After 15 minutes, detach the pan from the air fryer grill. Bring the foil packet to a cutting board and carefully unwrap it. Set the mushrooms and cooking liquid from the foil onto the sheet pan.

5. Place the basket on the toast position.

6. Select Toast, set the temperature to 350F (180C), and set the time for 15 minutes.

7. After about 10 minutes, detach the pan from the air fryer grill and stir the mushrooms. Return the pan to the air fryer grill and continue cooking for anywhere from 5 to 15 more minutes, or until the liquid is mostly gone and the mushrooms start to brown.

8. Serve immediately.

Nutrition: Calories 350 Fat 15 g Carbohydrates 3 g Sugar 1 g Protein 44 g Cholesterol 0 mg

Toasted Eggplant, Peppers, Garlic, and Onion

Preparation time: 15 minutes

Cooking time: 20 minutes

Servings 2

Ingredients:

- 1 small eggplant, halved and sliced
- 1 yellow bell pepper
- 1 red bell pepper
- 2 garlic cloves, quartered
- 1 red onion, sliced
- 1 tablespoon extra-virgin oil
- Salt and freshly black pepper
- 1/2 cup chopped fresh basil, for garnish
- Cooking spray

Directions:

1. Grease a nonstick baking dish with cooking spray.
2. Place the eggplant, garlic, red onion, and bell peppers in the greased baking dish. Set with the olive oil and toss to coat well. Spritz any uncoated surfaces with cooking spray.
3. Place the baking dish on the bake position.
4. Select Bake, set temperature to 350F (180C), and set time to 20 minutes.
5. Set the vegetables halfway through the cooking time.

6. When done, remove from the air fryer grill and sprinkle with salt and pepper.

7. Sprinkle the basil on top for garnish and serve.

Nutrition: Calories 184 Fat 11 g Carbohydrates 5 g Sugar 1 g Protein 12 g Cholesterol 0 mg

Garlicky Mixed Veggies

Preparation Time: 15 minutes

Cooking Time: 8 minutes

Servings: 4

Ingredients:

- 1 bunch fresh asparagus, trimmed
- 6 ounces fresh mushrooms, halved
- 6 Campari tomatoes, halved
- 1 red onion, cut into 1-inch chunks
- 3 garlic cloves, minced
- 2 tablespoons olive oil
- Salt and ground black pepper, as required

Directions:

1. In a large bowl, merge all ingredients and toss to coat well.

2. Place the water tray in the bottom of Smokeless Electric Grill.

3. Place about 2 cups of lukewarm water into the water tray.

4. Place the drip pan over water tray and then arrange the heating element.
5. Now, place the grilling pan over heating element.
6. Plugin the Smokeless Electric Grill and press the 'Power' button to turn it on.
7. Then press 'Fan" button.
8. Set the temperature settings according to manufacturer's directions.
9. Cover the grill with lid and let it preheat.
10. After preheating, remove the lid and grease the grilling pan.
11. Place the vegetables over the grilling pan.
12. Cover with the lid and cook for about 8 minutes, flipping occasionally.

Nutrition: Calories 137 Total Fat 7.7 g Saturated Fat 1.1 g Cholesterol 0 mg Sodium 54 mg Total Carbs 15.6 g Fiber 5.6 g Sugar 8.9 g Protein 5.8 g

Mediterranean Veggies

Preparation Time: 5 minutes

Cooking Time: 10 minutes

Servings: 4

Ingredients:

- 1 cup mixed bell peppers, chopped
- 1 cup eggplant, chopped
- 1 cup zucchini, chopped
- 1 cup mushrooms, chopped
- 1/2 cup onion, chopped
- 1/2 cup sun-dried tomato vinaigrette dressing

Directions:

1. In a large bowl, merge all ingredients and toss to coat well.
2. Refrigerate to marinate for about 1 hour.
3. Place the water tray in the bottom of Smokeless Electric Grill.

4. Place about 2 cups of lukewarm water into the water tray.

5. Place the drip pan over water tray and then arrange the heating element.

6. Now, place the grilling pan over heating element.

7. Plugin the Smokeless Electric Grill and press the 'Power' button to turn it on.

8. Then press 'Fan" button.

9. Set the temperature settings according to manufacturer's directions.

10. Cover the grill with lid and let it preheat.

11. After preheating, remove the lid and grease the grilling pan.

12. Place the vegetables over the grilling pan.

13. Cover with the lid and cook for about 8-10 minutes, flipping occasionally.

14. Serve hot.

Nutrition: Calories 159 Total Fat 11.2 g Saturated Fat 2 g Cholesterol 0 mg Sodium 336 mg Total Carbs 12.3 g Fiber 1.9 g Sugar 9.5 g Protein 1.6 g

Marinated Veggie Skewers

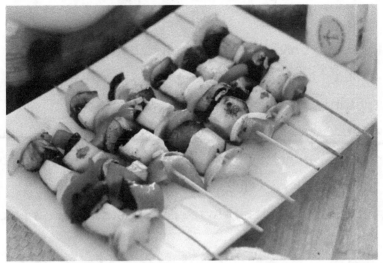

Preparation Time: 20 minutes

Cooking Time: 10 minutes

Servings: 4

Ingredients:

For Marinade:

- 2 garlic cloves, minced
- 2 teaspoons fresh basil, minced
- 2 teaspoons fresh oregano, minced
- 1/2 teaspoon cayenne pepper
- Sea Salt and ground black pepper
- 2 tablespoons fresh lemon juice
- 2 tablespoons olive oil

For Veggies:

- 2 large zucchinis, cut into thick slices
- 8 large button mushrooms, quartered

- 1 yellow bell pepper, seeded and cubed
- 1 red bell pepper, seeded and cubed

Directions:

1. For marinade: in a large bowl, attach all the ingredients and mix until well combined.
2. Bring the vegetables and toss to coat well.
3. Cover and refrigerate to marinate for at least 6-8 hours.
4. Remove the vegetables from the bowl and thread onto pre-soaked wooden skewers.
5. Place the water tray in the bottom of Smokeless Electric Grill.
6. Place about 2 cups of lukewarm water into the water tray.
7. Place the drip pan over water tray and then arrange the heating element.
8. Now, place the grilling pan over heating element.
9. Plugin the Smokeless Electric Grill and press the 'Power' button to turn it on.
10. Then press 'Fan" button.
11. Set the temperature settings according to manufacturer's directions. Cover the grill with lid and let it preheat.
12. After preheating, remove the lid and grease the grilling pan.
13. Place the skewers over the grilling pan. Cover with the lid and cook for about 8-10 minutes, flipping occasionally. Serve hot.

Nutrition: Calories 122 Total Fat 7.8 g Saturated Fat 1.2 g
Cholesterol 0 mg Sodium 81 mg Total Carbs 12.7 g Fiber 3.5 g
Sugar 6.8g Protein 4.3 g

Pineapple and Veggie Skewers

Preparation Time: 20 minutes

Cooking Time: 15 minutes

Servings: 6

Ingredients:

- 1/3 cup olive oil
- 11/2 teaspoons dried basil
- 1/3 teaspoon dried oregano
- Salt and ground black pepper, as required
- 2 zucchinis, cut into 1-inch slices
- 2 yellow squash, cut into 1-inch slices
- 1/2 pound whole fresh mushrooms
- 1 red bell pepper, cut into chunks
- 1 red onion, cut into chunks
- 12 cherry tomatoes

- 1 fresh pineapple, cut into chunks

Directions:

1. In a bowl, add oil, herbs, salt and black pepper and mix well.
2. Thread the veggies and pineapple onto pre-soaked wooden skewers.
3. Brush the veggies and pineapple with oil mixture evenly.
4. Place the water tray in the bottom of Smokeless Electric Grill.
5. Place about 2 cups of lukewarm water into the water tray.
6. Place the drip pan over water tray and then arrange the heating element.
7. Now, place the grilling pan over heating element.
8. Plugin the Smokeless Electric Grill and press the 'Power' button to turn it on.
9. Then press 'Fan" button.
10. Set the temperature settings according to manufacturer's directions.
11. Cover the grill with lid and let it preheat.
12. After preheating, remove the lid and grease the grilling pan.
13. Place the skewers over the grilling pan.
14. Cover with the lid and cook for about 10-15 minutes, flipping occasionally.
15. Serve hot.

Nutrition: Calories 220 Total Fat 11.9 g Saturated Fat 1.7 g Cholesterol 0 mg Sodium 47 mg Total Carbs 30 g Fiber 5 g Sugar 20.4 g Protein 4.3 g

Buttered Corn

Preparation Time: 10 minutes

Cooking Time: 20 minutes

Servings: 6

Ingredients:

- 6 fresh whole corn on the cob
- 1/2 cup butter, melted
- Salt, as required

Directions:

1. Husk the corn and detach all the silk.
2. Brush each corn with melted butter and sprinkle with salt.
3. Place the water tray in the bottom of Smokeless Electric Grill.
4. Place about 2 cups of lukewarm water into the water tray.
5. Place the drip pan over water tray and then arrange the heating element.
6. Now, place the grilling pan over heating element.
7. Plugin the Smokeless Electric Grill and press the 'Power' button to turn it on.
8. Then press 'Fan" button.
9. Set the temperature settings according to manufacturer's directions.
10. Cover the grill with lid and let it preheat.

11. After preheating, remove the lid and grease the grilling pan.

12. Place the corn over the grilling pan.

13. Cover with the lid and cook for about 20 minutes, rotating after every 5 minutes and brushing with butter once halfway through.

14. Serve warm.

Nutrition: Calories 268 Total Fat 17.2 g Saturated Fat 10 g Cholesterol 41 mg Sodium 159 mg Total Carbs 29 g Fiber 4.2 g Sugar 5 g Protein 5.2 g

Guacamole

Preparation Time: 15 minutes

Cooking Time: 4 minutes

Servings: 4

Ingredients:

- 2 ripe avocados, halved and pitted
- 2 teaspoons vegetable oil
- 3 tablespoons fresh lime juice
- 1 garlic clove, crushed
- 1/4 teaspoon ground chipotle chili
- Salt, as required
- 1/4 cup red onion, chopped finely
- 1/4 cup fresh cilantro, chopped finely

Directions:

1. Brush the cut sides of each avocado half with oil.
2. Place the water tray in the bottom of Smokeless Electric Grill.
3. Place about 2 cups of lukewarm water into the water tray.
4. Place the drip pan over water tray and then arrange the heating element.
5. Now, place the grilling pan over heating element.
6. Plugin the Smokeless Electric Grill and press the 'Power' button to turn it on.
7. Then press 'Fan" button.

8. Set the temperature settings according to manufacturer's directions.

9. Cover the grill with lid and let it preheat.

10. After preheating, remove the lid and grease the grilling pan.

11. Place the avocado halves over the grilling pan, cut side down.

12. Cook, uncovered for about 2-4 minutes.

13. Transfer the avocados onto cutting board and let them cool slightly.

14. Remove the peel and transfer the flesh into a bowl.

15. Add the lime juice, garlic, chipotle and salt and with a fork, mash until almost smooth.

16. Stir in onion and cilantro and refrigerate, covered for about 1 hour before serving.

Nutrition: Calories 230 Total Fat 21.9 g Saturated Fat 4.6g Cholesterol 0 mg Sodium 46 mg Total Carbs 9.7 g Fiber 6.9 g Sugar 0.8 g Protein 2.1 g

Tofu Nuggets

Preparation Time: 15 minutes

Cooking Time: 25 minutes

Servings: 4

Ingredients:

- Tofu
- 14 oz. tofu, sliced into cubes
- Cooking spray
- 1/4 cup flour
- 1 teaspoon garlic powder
- 1/2 teaspoon paprika
- 1/2 teaspoon ground cumin
- Salt to taste
- Sauce
- 1 tablespoon avocado oil
- 2 tablespoons sugar
- 3 tablespoons soy sauce
- 2 tablespoons honey
- 1 teaspoon garlic powder
- 1 tablespoon ginger, grated
- Pepper to taste

Directions:

1. Spray tofu cubes with oil.
2. Mix remaining ingredients in a bowl.
3. Coat tofu evenly with this mixture.

4. Add the tofu cubes to the air fryer.

5. Set it to air fry.

6. Cook at 350 degrees F for 10 minutes.

7. Toss and cook for 15 minutes.

8. In a bowl, mix the sauce ingredients.

9. Toss the tofu in the sauce and serve.

Nutrition: Calories 356 Fat 8.7 g Carbohydrates 1.4 g   Sugar 0.2 g Protein 62.2 g Cholesterol 153 mg

Zucchini Lasagna

Preparation Time: 15 minutes

Cooking Time: 15 minutes

Servings: 4

Ingredients:

- 1 zucchini, sliced thinly lengthwise and divided
- 1/2 cup marinara sauce, divided
- 1/4 cup ricotta, divided
- 1 cup fresh basil leaves,
- 1/4 cup spinach leaves, chopped and divided

Directions:

1. Set half of the zucchini slices in a small loaf pan.
2. Spread with half of marinara sauce and ricotta.
3. Top with half of spinach and basil.
4. Repeat layers with the remaining ingredients.

5. Cover the pan with foil.

6. Place inside the air fryer.

7. Set it to bake.

8. Cook at 400 F

9. Remove foil and cook for another 5 minutes.

Nutrition: Calories 233 Fat 7.9 g Carbohydrates 3.2 g Sugar 0.1 g Protein 35.6 g Cholesterol 32 mg

Veggie Rolls

Preparation Time: 20 minutes

Cooking Time: 20 minutes

Servings: 5

Ingredients:

- 1 tablespoon olive oil
- 1 clove garlic, minced
- 1 teaspoon ginger, minced
- 3 scallions, chopped
- 1/2 lb. mushrooms, chopped
- 2 cups cabbage, chopped

- 8 oz. water chestnuts, diced
- Salt and pepper to taste
- 6 spring roll wrappers
- 1 tablespoon water

Directions:

1. Attach oil to a pan over medium heat.
2. Cook the garlic, ginger, scallions and mushrooms for 2 minutes.
3. Stir in the remaining vegetables.
4. Season with salt and pepper.
5. Cook for 3 minutes, stirring.
6. Transfer to a strainer.
7. Add vegetables on top of the wrappers.
8. Roll up the wrappers.
9. Seal the edges with water.
10. Place the rolls inside the air fryer.
11. Choose air fry setting.
12. Cook at 360 F for 15 minutes.

Nutrition: Calories 155 Fat 2 g Carbohydrates 6 g Sugar 2 g Protein 25 g Cholesterol 0 mg

Onion Rings

Preparation Time: 10 minutes

Cooking Time: 10 minutes

Servings: 3

Ingredients:

- 2 white onions, sliced into rings
- 1 cup flour
- 2 eggs, beaten
- 1 cup breadcrumbs

Directions:

1. Cover the onion rings with flour.
2. Dip in the egg.
3. Dredge with breadcrumbs.
4. Add to the air fryer.
5. Set it to air fry.
6. Cook at 400 F for 10 minutes.

Nutrition: Calories: 524 Carbohydrates: 65g Fiber: 4g
Protein: 33g

Cheesy Egg Rolls

Preparation Time: 15 minutes

Cooking Time: 12 minutes

Servings: 12

Ingredients:

- 12 spring roll wrappers
- 12 slices provolone cheese
- 3 eggs, cooked and sliced
- 1 carrot, sliced into thin strips
- 1 tablespoon water

Directions:

1. Top the wrappers with cheese, eggs and carrot strips.
2. Roll up the wrappers and seal with water.
3. Place inside the air fryer.
4. Set it to air fry.
5. Cook at 390 degrees F for 12 minutes, turning once or twice.

Nutrition: Calories 356 Fat 18g Carbohydrates 5 g Protein 34g;

Cauliflower Bites

Preparation Time: 15 minutes

Cooking Time: 10 minutes

Servings: 6

Ingredients:

Cauliflower bites

- 4 cups cauliflower rice
- 1 egg, beaten
- 1 cup Parmesan cheese, grated
- 1 cup cheddar, shredded
- 2 tablespoons chives, chopped

- 1/4 cup breadcrumbs
- Salt and pepper to taste

Sauce

- 1/2 cup ketchup
- 2 tablespoons hot sauce

Directions:

1. Combine cauliflower bites ingredients in a bowl.
2. Mix well.
3. Form balls from the mixture.
4. Choose air fry setting.
5. Add cauliflower bites to the air fryer.
6. Cook at 375 F for 10 minutes.
7. Mix ketchup and hot sauce.
8. Serve cauliflower bites with dip.

Nutrition: Calories 285   Fat 12.8 g   Carbohydrates 3.7 g
Protein 38.1 g;

Baked Potatoes

Preparation Time: 20 minutes

Cooking Time: 45 minutes

Servings: 6

Ingredients:

- 6 potatoes
- 1 tablespoon olive oil
- Salt to taste
- 1 cup butter
- 1/2 cup milk
- 1/2 cup sour cream
- 1 1/2 cup cheddar, shredded and divided

Directions:

1. Poke the potatoes using a fork.
2. Add to the air fryer.
3. Set it to bake.
4. Cook at 400 F for 40 minutes.

5. Take out of the oven.

6. Slice the potato in half

7. Scoop out the potato flesh.

8. Mix potato flesh with the remaining ingredients.

9. Put the mixture back to the potato shells.

10. Bake in the air fryer for 5 minutes.

Nutrition: Calories 302 Fat 20 g Carbohydrates 8 g Sugar 2 g Protein 24 g Cholesterol 142 mg

Vegetarian Pizza

Preparation Time: 15 minutes

Cooking Time: 10 minutes

Servings: 1

Ingredients:

- 1 pizza crust
- 1 tablespoon olive oil
- 1/4 cup tomato sauce
- 1 cup mushrooms
- 1/2 cup black olives, sliced
- 1 clove garlic, minced
- 1/2 teaspoon oregano
- Salt and pepper to taste
- 1 cup mozzarella, shredded

Directions:

1. Brush pizza crust with oil.

2. Spread tomato sauce on top.

3. Arrange mushrooms and olives on top.

4. Sprinkle with garlic and oregano.

5. Season with salt and pepper.

6. Top with mozzarella cheese.

7. Place inside the air fryer.

8. Set it to bake.

9. Cook at 400 F for 10 minutes.

Nutrition: Calories 260 Fat 13 g Carbohydrates 1 g Sugar 0 g Protein 35 g Cholesterol 142 mg

Brussels Sprout Chips

Preparation Time: 10 minutes

Cooking Time: 15 minutes

Servings: 2

Ingredients:

- 2 cups Brussels sprouts, sliced thinly
- 1 tablespoon olive oil
- 1 teaspoon garlic powder
- Salt and pepper to taste
- 2 tablespoons Parmesan cheese, grated

Directions:

1. Toss the Brussels sprouts in oil.
2. Sprinkle with garlic powder, salt, pepper and Parmesan cheese.
3. Choose bake function.
4. Add the Brussels sprouts in the air fryer.
5. Cook at 350 degrees F for 8 minutes.

6. Flip and cook for 7 more minutes.

Nutrition: Calories 175 Fat 5 g Carbohydrates 3 g Sugar 0.2 g Protein 27 g Cholesterol 0 mg

Air Fryer Asparagus

Preparation Time: 5 minutes

Cooking Time: 8 minutes

Servings: 2

Ingredients:

- **Nutrition:**al yeast
- Olive oil non-stick spray
- One bunch of asparagus

Directions:s

1. Wash asparagus and then trim off thick, woody ends.
2. Spray asparagus with olive oil spray and sprinkle with yeast.
3. Add the asparagus to air fryer rack/basket in a singular layer. Set temperature to 360°F, and set time to 8 minutes. Select START/STOP to begin.

Nutrition: Calories: 17 Fat: 4g Protein: 9g Carbs: 4 g.

Almond Flour Battered and Crisped Onion Rings

Preparation Time: 5 minutes

Cooking Time: 15 minutes

Servings: 3

Ingredients:

- 1/2 cup almond flour
- 1/3 cup coconut milk
- 1 big white onion, sliced into rings
- 1 egg, beaten
- 1 tablespoon baking powder
- 1 tablespoon smoked paprika
- Salt and pepper to taste

Directions:s

1. Preheat the air fryer Oven for 5 minutes.
2. In a mixing bowl, mix the almond flour, baking powder, smoked paprika, salt and pepper.
3. In another bowl, combine the eggs and coconut milk.
4. Soak the onion slices into the egg mixture.
5. Dredge the onion slices in the almond flour mixture.
6. Pour into the Oven rack/basket. Set temperature to 325°F, and set time to 15 minutes. Select START/STOP to begin. Shake the fryer basket for even cooking.

Nutrition: Calories: 217 Fat: 17.9g Protein: 5.3g Carbs:

Asparagus Strata

Preparation Time: 10 minutes

Cooking Time: 17 minutes

Servings: 4

Ingredients:

- 6 asparagus spears, cut into 2-inch pieces
- 2 slices whole-wheat bread, cut into 1/2-inch cubes
- 4 eggs
- 3 tablespoons whole milk
- 1/2 cup grated Havarti or Swiss cheese
- 2 tablespoons chopped flat-leaf parsley
- Pinch salt
- Freshly ground black pepper

Directions:s

1. Place the asparagus spears and 1 tablespoon water in a 6-inch baking pan and place in the Air fryer basket Oven.

2. Bake until crisp and tender. Detach the asparagus from the pan and drain it. Spray the pan with nonstick cooking spray. Arrange the bread cubes and asparagus into the pan and set aside. In a medium bowl, beat the eggs with the milk until combined. Add the cheese, parsley, salt, and pepper. Pour into the baking pan. Set temperature to 360°F, and set time to 14 minutes or until the eggs are set and the top starts to brown. Select START/STOP to begin.

Nutrition: Calories: 166 Fat: 49g Protein: 12g Fiber: 2g Carbs: 1.3 g

Jalapeño Poppers

Preparation Time: 10 minutes

Cooking Time: 10 minutes

Servings: 4

Ingredients:

- 12-18 whole fresh jalapeño
- 1 cup nonfat refried beans
- 1 cup shredded Monterey Jack cheese
- 1 scallion, sliced
- 1 teaspoon salt, divided
- 1/4 cup all-purpose flour
- 2 large eggs
- 1/2 cup fine cornmeal
- Olive oil or canola oil cooking spray

Directions:s

1. Start by slicing each jalapeño lengthwise on one side. Place the jalapeños side by side in a microwave safe bowl and microwave them until they are slightly soft; usually around 5 minutes.

2. While your jalapeños cook; mix refried beans, scallions, 1/2 teaspoon salt, and cheese in a bowl.

3. Once your jalapeños are softened you can scoop out the seeds and add one tablespoon of your refried bean mixture (It can be a little less if the pepper is smaller.) Press the jalapeño closed around the filling.

4. Set your eggs in a small bowl and place your flour in a separate bowl. In a third bowl mix your cornmeal and the remaining salt in a third bowl.

5. Roll each pepper in the flour, then dip it in the egg, and finally roll it in the cornmeal making sure to coat the entire pepper.

6. Place the peppers on a flat surface and coat them with a cooking spray; olive oil cooking spray is suggested.

7. Pour into the Oven rack/basket. Place the Rack on the middle-shelf of the Air fryer oven. Set temperature to 400°F, and set time to 5 minutes. Select START/STOP to begin. Turn each pepper and then cook for another 5 minutes; serve hot.

Nutrition: Calories: 244 Fat: 12g Protein: 12g Fiber: 2.4g Carbs: 4.1 g

Parmesan Breaded Zucchini Chips

Preparation Time: 15 minutes

Cooking Time: 20 minutes

Servings: 4

Ingredients:

For the zucchini chips:

- 2 medium zucchini
- 2 eggs
- 1/3 cup bread crumbs
- 1/3 cup grated Parmesan cheese
- Salt
- Pepper
- Cooking oil

For the lemon aioli:

- 1/2 cup mayonnaise

- 1/2 tablespoon olive oil
- Juice of 1/2 lemon
- 1 teaspoon minced garlic
- Salt
- Pepper

Directions:s

To make the zucchini chips:

1. Slice the zucchini into thin chips (about 1/8 inch thick) using a knife or mandolin.
2. In a small bowl, beat the eggs. In another small bowl, combine the bread crumbs, Parmesan cheese, and salt and pepper to taste.
3. Spray the air fryer basket with cooking oil.
4. Dip the zucchini slices one at a time in the eggs and then the bread crumb mixture. You can also sprinkle the bread crumbs onto the zucchini slices with a spoon.
5. Place the zucchini chips in the air fryer basket, but do not stack.
6. Pour into the Oven rack/basket. Place the Rack on the middle-shelf of the Air fryer oven. Cook in batches. Spray the chips with cooking oil from a distance (otherwise, the breading may fly off). Cook for 10 minutes.
7. Remove the cooked zucchini chips from the air fryer oven, and then repeat with the remaining zucchini.

To make the lemon aioli:

1. While the zucchini is cooking, combine the mayonnaise, olive oil, lemon juice, and garlic in a small bowl, adding salt and pepper to taste. Mix well until fully combined.
2. Cool the zucchini and serve alongside the aioli.

Nutrition: Calories: 192 Fat: 13g Protein: 6g Fiber: 4g Carbs: 2.3 g

Bell Pepper-Corn Wrapped in Tortilla

Preparation Time: 3 minutes

Cooking Time: 15 minutes

Servings: 4

Ingredients:

- 1 small red bell pepper, chopped
- 1 small yellow onion, diced
- 1 tablespoon water
- 2 cobs grilled corn kernels
- 4 large tortillas
- 4 pieces commercial vegan nuggets, chopped
- mixed greens for garnish

Directions:

1. Preheat the air fryer oven to 400F.
2. In a skillet heated over medium heat, water sauté the vegan nuggets together with the onions, bell peppers, and corn kernels. Set aside.

3. Place filling inside the corn tortillas.

4. Pour the tortillas into the Oven rack/basket. Place the Rack on the middle-shelf of the Air fryer oven. Set temperature to 400F, and set time to 15 minutes until the tortilla wraps are crispy.

5. Serve with mix greens on top.

Nutrition: Calories: 548 Fat: 20.7g Protein: 46g Carbs: 1.2 g

Baked Cheesy Eggplant with Marinara

Preparation Time: 5 minutes

Cooking Time: 45 minutes

Servings: 3

Ingredients:

- 1 clove garlic, sliced
- 1 large eggplants
- 1 tablespoon olive oil
- 1 tablespoon olive oil
- 1/2 pinch salt, or as needed
- 1/4 cup and 2 tablespoons bread crumbs
- 1/4 cup and 2 tablespoons ricotta cheese
- 1/4 cup grated Parmesan cheese
- 1/4 cup grated Parmesan cheese
- 1/4 cup water, plus more as needed

- 1/4 teaspoon red pepper flakes
- 1-1/2 cups prepared marinara sauce
- 1-1/2 teaspoons olive oil
- 2 tablespoons shredded pepper jack cheese
- salt and freshly black pepper

Directions:s

1. Cut eggplant crosswise in 5 pieces. Peel and chop two pieces into 1/2-inch cubes.
2. Lightly grease baking pan of air fryer with 1 tbsp. olive oil for 5 minutes, heat oil at 390°F. Add half eggplant strips and cook for 2 minutes per side. Transfer to a plate.
3. Add 1 1/2 tsp. olive oil and add garlic. Cook for a minute. Add chopped eggplants. Season with pepper flakes and salt. Cook for 4 minutes. Lower heat to 330F. And continue cooking eggplants until soft, around 8 minutes more.
4. Stir in water and marinara sauce. Cook for 7 minutes until heated through. Stirring every now and then. Transfer to a bowl.
5. In a bowl, whisk well pepper, salt, pepper jack cheese, Parmesan cheese, and ricotta. Evenly spread cheeses over eggplant strips and then fold in half.
6. Lay folded eggplant in baking pan. Pour marinara sauce on top.

7. In a small bowl whisk well olive oil, and bread crumbs. Sprinkle all over sauce.

8. Place the baking dish in the Air fryer oven cooking basket. Cook for 15 minutes at 390°F until tops are lightly browned.

9. Serve and enjoy.

Nutrition: Calories: 405 Fat: 21.4g Protein: 12.7g Carbs: 3.6 g

Spicy Sweet Potato Fries

Preparation Time: 5 minutes

Cooking Time: 37 minutes

Servings4 2

Ingredients:

- 2 tbsp. sweet potato fry seasoning mix
- 2 tbsp. olive oil
- 2 sweet potatoes
- Seasoning Mix:
- 2 tbsp. salt
- 1 tbsp. cayenne pepper
- 1 tbsp. dried oregano
- 1 tbsp. fennel
- 2 tbsp. coriander

Directions:

1. Slice both ends off sweet potatoes and peel. Slice lengthwise in half and again crosswise to make four pieces from each potato.

2. Slice each potato piece into 2-3 slices, and then slice into fries.
3. Grind together all of seasoning mix ingredients and mix in the salt.
4. Ensure the air fryer oven is preheated to 350 degrees.
5. Toss potato pieces in olive oil, sprinkling with seasoning mix and tossing well to coat thoroughly.
6. Add fries to air fryer basket. Set temperature to 350F, and set time to 27 minutes. Select START/STOP to begin.
7. Take out the basket and turn fries. Turn off air fryer and let cook 10-12 minutes till fries are golden.

Nutrition: Calories: 89 Fat: 14g Protein: 8g Sugar: 3g Carbs: 0.4 g

Creamy Spinach Quiche

Preparation Time: 10 minutes

Cooking Time: 20 minutes

Servings: 4

Ingredients:

- Premade quiche crust, chilled and rolled flat to a 7-inch round
- 2 eggs
- 1/4 cup of milk
- Pinch of salt and pepper
- 1 clove of garlic
- 1/2 cup of cooked spinach, drained and coarsely chopped
- 1/4 cup of shredded mozzarella cheese
- 1/4 cup of shredded cheddar cheese

Directions:

1. Preheat the air fryer oven to 360 degrees.

2. Press the premade crust into a 7-inch pie tin, or any appropriately sized glass or ceramic heat-safe dish. Press and trim at the edges if necessary. With a fork, pierce several holes in the dough to allow air circulation and prevent cracking of the crust while cooking.

3. In a mixing bowl, beat the eggs until fluffy and until the yolks and white are evenly combined.

4. Add milk, garlic, spinach, salt and pepper, and half the cheddar and mozzarella cheese to the eggs. Set the rest of the cheese aside for now, and stir the mixture until completely blended. Make sure the spinach is not clumped together, but rather spread among the other ingredients.

5. Pour the mixture into the pie crust, slowly and carefully to avoid splashing. The mixture should almost fill the crust, but not completely – leaving a 1/4 inch of crust at the edges.

6. Place the baking dish in the Air fryer oven cooking basket. Set the air fryer oven timer for 15 minutes. After15 minutes, the air fryer will shut off, and the quiche will already be firm and the crust beginning to brown. Sprinkle the rest of the cheddar and mozzarella cheese on top of the quiche filling. Reset the air fryer oven at 360 degrees for 5 minutes. After 5 minutes, when the air fryer shuts off, the cheese will have formed an exquisite crust on top and the quiche will be golden brown and perfect. Remove from the air fryer using oven mitts or tongs, and set on a heat-safe surface to cool for a few minutes before cutting.

Nutrition: Calories 254   Fat 14.2 g   Carbohydrates 5.7 g Protein 39.1 g;

Air Fryer Cauliflower Rice

Preparation Time: 5 minutes

Cooking Time: 20 minutes

Servings: 4

Ingredients:

- 1 tsp. turmeric
- 1 C. diced carrot
- 1/2 C. diced onion
- 2 tbsp. low-sodium soy sauce
- 1/2 block of extra firm tofu
- 1/2 C. frozen peas
- 2 minced garlic cloves
- 1/2 C. chopped broccoli
- 1 tbsp. minced ginger

- 1 tbsp. rice vinegar
- 1 1/2 tsp. toasted sesame oil
- 2 tbsp. reduced-sodium soy sauce
- 3 C. riced cauliflower

Directions:

1. Crumble tofu in a large bowl and toss with all the Round one ingredient.
2. Preheat the air fryer oven to 370 degrees, place the baking dish in the Air fryer oven cooking basket, set temperature to 370F, and set time to 10 minutes and cook 10 minutes, making sure to shake once.
3. In another bowl, toss ingredients from Round 2 together.
4. Add Round 2 mixture to air fryer and cook another 10 minutes, ensuring to shake 5 minutes in.
5. Enjoy!

Nutrition: Calories: 67 Fat: 8g Protein: 3g Carbs: 1 g

Brown Rice, Spinach and Tofu Frittata

Preparation Time: 5 minutes

Cooking Time: 55 minutes

Servings: 4

Ingredients:

- 1/2 cup baby spinach, chopped
- 1/2 cup kale, chopped
- 1/2 onion, chopped
- 1/2 teaspoon turmeric
- 1 1/3 cups brown rice, cooked
- 1 flax egg
- 1 package firm tofu
- 1 tablespoon olive oil
- 1 yellow pepper, chopped
- 2 tablespoons soy sauce

- 2 teaspoons arrowroot powder
- 2 teaspoons Dijon mustard
- 2/3 cup almond milk
- 3 big mushrooms, chopped
- 3 tablespoons nutritional yeast
- 4 cloves garlic, crushed
- 4 spring onions, chopped
- a handful of basil leaves, chopped

Directions:

1. Preheat the air fryer oven to 375F. Grease a pan that will fit inside the air fryer oven.

2. Prepare the frittata crust by mixing the brown rice and flax egg. Press the rice onto the baking dish until you form a crust. Brush with a little oil and cook for 10 minutes.

3. Meanwhile, heat olive oil in a skillet over medium flame and sauté the garlic and onions for 2 minutes.

4. Add the pepper and mushroom and continue stirring for 3 minutes.

5. Stir in the kale, spinach, spring onions, and basil. Remove from the pan and set aside.

6. In a food processor, press together the tofu, mustard, turmeric, soy sauce, nutritional yeast, vegan milk and arrowroot powder. Pour in a mixing bowl and stir in the sautéed vegetables.

7. Pour the vegan frittata mixture over the rice crust and cook in the air fryer oven for 40 minutes.

Nutrition: Calories: 226 Fat: 8.05g Protein: 10.6g Carbs: 5 g

Stuffed Mushrooms

Preparation Time: 7 minutes

Cooking Time: 8 minutes

Servings: 12

Ingredients:

- 2 Rashers Bacon, Diced
- 1/2 Onion, Diced
- 1/2 Bell Pepper, Diced
- 1 Small Carrot, Diced
- 24 Medium Size Mushrooms (Separate the caps and stalks)
- 1 cup Shredded Cheddar Plus Extra for the Top
- 1/2 cup Sour Cream

Directions:

1. Chop the mushrooms stalks finely into the Oven rack/basket. Place the Rack on the middle-shelf of the Air fryer oven. Set temperature to 350F, and set time to 8 minutes and fry them up with the bacon, onion, pepper and carrot. When the veggies are fairly tender, stir in the sour cream and the cheese. Keep on the heat until the cheese has melted and everything is mixed nicely.
2. Now grab the mushroom caps and heap a plop of filling on each one.
3. Place in the fryer basket and top with a little extra cheese.

Nutrition: Calories 260 Fat 13 g Carbohydrates 1 g Sugar 0 g Protein 35 g Cholesterol 142 mg

Air Fried Carrots, Yellow Squash and Zucchini

Preparation Time: 5 minutes

Cooking Time: 35 minutes

Servings: 4

Ingredients:

- 1 tbsp. chopped tarragon leaves
- 1/2 tsp. white pepper
- 1 tsp. salt
- 1 pound yellow squash
- 1 pound zucchini
- 6 tsp. olive oil
- 1/2 pound carrots

Directions:

1. Stem and root the end of squash and zucchini and cut in 1/3-inch half-moons. Peel and cut carrots into 1-inch cubes

2. Merge carrot cubes with 2 teaspoons of olive oil, tossing to combine.

3. Pour into the air fryer oven basket, set temperature to 400F, and set time to 5 minutes.

4. As carrots cook, drizzle remaining olive oil over squash and zucchini pieces, then season with pepper and salt. Toss well to coat.

5. Add squash and zucchini when the timer for carrots goes off. Cook 30 minutes, making sure to toss 2-3 times during the cooking process.

6. Once done, take out veggies and toss with tarragon. Serve up warm.

Nutrition: Calories: 122 Fat: 9g Protein: 6g Carbs: 5g

Winter Vegetarian Frittata

Preparation Time: 5 minutes

Cooking Time: 30 minutes

Servings: 4

Ingredients:

- 1 leek, peeled and thinly sliced into rings
- 2 cloves garlic, finely minced
- 3 medium-sized carrots, finely chopped
- 2 tablespoons olive oil
- 6 large-sized eggs
- Sea salt and ground black pepper
- 1/2 teaspoon dried marjoram, finely minced
- 1/2 cup yellow cheese of choice

Directions:

1. Sauté the leek, garlic, and carrot in hot olive oil until they are tender and fragrant; reserve.

2. In the meantime, preheat your air fryer oven to 330 degrees F.

3. In a bowl, merge the eggs along with the salt, ground black pepper, and marjoram.

4. Then, grease the inside of your baking dish with a nonstick cooking spray. Pour the whisked eggs into the baking dish. Stir in the sautéed carrot mixture. Top with the cheese shreds.

5. Place the baking dish in the air fryer oven cooking basket. Cook about 30 minutes and serve warm.

Nutrition: Calories 302 Fat 20 g Carbohydrates 8 g Sugar 2 g Protein 24 g Cholesterol 142 mg

Brussels sprouts with Balsamic Oil

Preparation Time: 5 minutes

Cooking Time: 15 minutes

Servings: 4

Ingredients:

- 1/4 teaspoon salt
- 1 tablespoon balsamic vinegar
- 2 cups Brussels sprouts, halved
- 1 tablespoons olive oil

Directions:

1. Preheat the air fryer oven for 5 minutes.
2. Mix all ingredients in a bowl until the zucchini fries are well coated.
3. Place in the air fryer oven basket.
4. Close and cook for 15 minutes for 350F.

Nutrition: Calories: 82 Fat: 6.8g Protein: 1.5g Carbs: 4.3 g

Buttery Pepperoni Grilled Cheese Sandwich

Preparation Time: 5 minutes

Cooking Time: 5 minutes

Servings: 2

Ingredients:

- 4 slices of Bread
- 4 slices of Mozzarella Cheese
- 4 tbsp. Butter
- 18 Pepperoni Slices

Directions:

1. Preheat your grill to medium-high.
2. Meanwhile, set each slice of bread with a tablespoon of butter. It seems like too much, but the taste is just incredible.

3. Divide the mozzarella and pepperoni among the insides of two bread slices.
4. Top the sandwich with the other slices of bread, keeping the buttery side up.
5. When the green light appears, open the grill.
6. Place the sandwiches carefully onto the bottom plate.
7. Lower the lid, and gently press.
8. Allow the sandwich to cook for 4-5 minutes.
9. Open the lid, transfer to a serving plate, cut in half, and serve. Enjoy!

Nutrition: Calories 625 Total Fats 46g Carbs 29g Protein 22g Fiber: 2g

Cheesy Buffalo Avocado Sandwich

Preparation Time: 5 minutes

Cooking Time: 4 minutes

Servings: 4

Ingredients:

- 1 Avocado
- 2 Bread Slices
- 2 slices Cheddar Cheese
- 1 tbsp. Butter
- Buffalo Sauce:
- 4 tbsp. Hot Sauce
- 1 tbs. White Vinegar

- 1/4 cup Butter
- 1/4 tsp. Salt
- 1 tsp. Cayenne Pepper
- 1/4 tsp. Garlic Salt

Directions:

1. Preheat your grill to 375 degrees F.
2. Meanwhile, peel the avocado, scoop out the flash, and mash it with a fork.
3. Spread the avocado onto a bread slice, and top with the cheddar cheese.
4. Spread the butter onto the outside of the other bread slice.
5. Top the sandwich with the buttery slice, with the butter-side up.
6. Grease the bottom cooking plate and place the sandwich there, with the butter-side up.
7. Lower the lid, press, and let the sandwich grill for about 4 minutes.
8. Meanwhile, merge together all of the sauce ingredients.
9. Serve the sandwich with the Buffalo sauce and enjoy!

Nutrition: Calories 485 Total Fats 24g Carbs 35g Protein 8g Fiber: 3g

Avocado Egg Rolls

Preparation Time: 5 minutes

Cooking Time: 5 minutes

Servings: 5

Ingredients:

- 10 egg roll wrappers
- 3 avocados, peeled and pitted
- 1 tomato, diced
- Salt and ground black pepper, to taste
- Cooking spray

Directions:

1. Set the air fryer basket with cooking spray.
2. Put the tomato and avocados in a food processor. Sprinkle with salt and ground black pepper. Pulse to mix and coarsely mash until smooth.
3. Unfold the wrappers on a clean work surface, and then divide the mixture in the center of each wrapper. Roll the wrapper up and press to seal.

4. Transfer the rolls to the basket and spritz with cooking spray.

5. Slide the basket into the air fryer. Cook at the corresponding preset mode or Air Fry at 350F (180C) for 5 minutes.

6. Set the rolls halfway through the cooking time.

7. When cooked, the rolls should be golden brown.

8. Serve immediately.

Nutrition: Calories: 17 Fat: 4g Protein: 9g Carbs: 4 g.

Baja Cod Tacos with Mango Salsa

Preparation time: 15 minutes

Cooking time: 17 minutes

Servings 6 tacos

Ingredients

- 1 egg
- 5 ounces (142 g) Mexican beer
- 1/3 cup all-purpose flour
- 1/3 cup cornstarch
- 1/4 teaspoon chili powder
- 1/2 teaspoon ground cumin
- 1/2 pound (227 g) cod, cut into large pieces
- 6 corn tortillas
- Cooking spray

Salsa:

- 1 mango, peeled and diced
- 1/4 red bell pepper, diced

- 1/2 small jalapeño, diced
- 1/4 red onion, minced
- Juice of half a lime
- Pinch chopped fresh cilantro
- 1/4 teaspoon salt
- 1/4 teaspoon ground black pepper

Directions:

1. Set the air fryer basket with cooking spray.
2. Whisk the egg with beer in a bowl. Combine the flour, cornstarch, chili powder, and cumin in a separate bowl.
3. Dredge the cod in the egg mixture first, then in the flour mixture to coat well. Shake the excess off.
4. Arrange the cod in the air fryer basket and spritz with cooking spray.
5. Slide the basket into the air fryer. Cook at the corresponding preset mode or Air Fry at 380F (193C) for 17 minutes.
6. Flip the cod halfway through the cooking time.
7. When cooked, the cod should be golden brown and crunchy.
8. Meanwhile, merge the ingredients for the salsa in a small bowl. Stir to mix well.
9. Unfold the tortillas on a clean work surface, then divide the fish on the tortillas and spread the salsa on top. Fold to serve.

Nutrition: Calories 155 Fat 2 g Carbohydrates 6 g Sugar 2 g
Protein 25 g Cholesterol 0 mg

Black Bean and Sweet Potato Burritos

Preparation time: 15 minutes

Cooking time: 30 minutes

Servings 6

Ingredients

- 2 sweet potatoes
- 1 tablespoon vegetable oil
- Kosher salt and black pepper, to taste
- 6 large flour tortillas
- 1 (16-ounce / 454-g) can refried black beans, divided
- 11/2 cups baby spinach, divided
- 6 eggs, scrambled
- 1/3 cup grated Cheddar cheese, divided
- 1/4 cup salsa
- 1/4 cup sour cream
- Cooking spray

Directions:

1. Set the sweet potatoes in a large bowl, then drizzle with vegetable oil and sprinkle with salt and black pepper. Toss to coat well.
2. Put the potatoes in the air fryer basket.
3. Slide the basket into the air fryer. Cook at the corresponding preset mode or Air Fry at 400F (205C) for 10 minutes.
4. Set the potatoes halfway through the cooking time.
5. When done, the potatoes should be lightly browned. Remove the potatoes from the air fryer.
6. Unfold the tortillas on a clean work surface. Divide the black beans, spinach, air fried sweet potatoes, scrambled eggs, and cheese on top of the tortillas.
7. Fold the long side of the tortillas over the filling, and then fold in the shorter side to wrap the filling to make the burritos.
8. Wrap the burritos in the aluminum foil and put in the basket.
9. Slide the basket into the air fryer. Cook at the corresponding preset mode or Air Fry at 350F (180C) for 20 minutes. Flip the burritos halfway through the cooking time.
10. Remove the burritos from the air fryer and spread with sour cream and salsa. Serve immediately.

Nutrition: Calories 260 Fat 13 g Carbohydrates 1 g Sugar 0 g
Protein 35 g Cholesterol 142 mg

Conversion Tables

The unit of measure conversion table is essential in the kitchen when you want to prepare a recipe measured according to a standard different from what you are used to

The recipes are all expressed according to the decimal metric system, but some readers may need to transform them into local measurement systems.

Indeed, some mathematics may be needed initially, but even more, a little logic is necessary because a cup of liquids will weigh differently from a cup of solids, and the same happens with ounces that can measure solid and liquid ingredients.

COOKING CONVERSION CHART

Measurement

CUP	ONCES	MILLILITERS	TABLESPOONS
8 cup	64 oz	1895 ml	128
6 cup	48 oz	1420 ml	96
5 cup	40 oz	1180 ml	80
4 cup	32 oz	960 ml	64
2 cup	16 oz	480 ml	32
1 cup	8 oz	240 ml	16
3/4 cup	6 oz	177 ml	12
2/3 cup	5 oz	158 ml	11
1/2 cup	4 oz	118 ml	8
3/8 cup	3 oz	90 ml	6
1/3 cup	2.5 oz	79 ml	5.5
1/4 cup	2 oz	59 ml	4
1/8 cup	1 oz	30 ml	3
1/16 cup	1/2 oz	15 ml	1

Temperature

FAHRENHEIT	CELSIUS
100 °F	37 °C
150 °F	65 °C
200 °F	93 °C
250 °F	121 °C
300 °F	150 °C
325 °F	160 °C
350 °F	180 °C
375 °F	190 °C
400 °F	200 °C
425 °F	220 °C
450 °F	230 °C
500 °F	260 °C
525 °F	274 °C
550 °F	288 °C

Weight

IMPERIAL	METRIC
1/2 oz	15 g
1 oz	29 g
2 oz	57 g
3 oz	85 g
4 oz	113 g
5 oz	141 g
6 oz	170 g
8 oz	227 g
10 oz	283 g
12 oz	340 g
13 oz	369 g
14 oz	397 g
15 oz	425 g
1 lb	453 g

CPSIA information can be obtained
at www.ICGtesting.com
Printed in the USA
BVHW090220180122
626423BV00011B/347

9 781803 123530